THE MIDDLE AGES IN THE ATHENIAN AGORA

AMERICAN SCHOOL OF CLASSICAL STUDIES
AT ATHENS

PRINCETON · NEW JERSEY

1961

1. Late Roman Wall, the Acropolis in the Background.

Classical civilization in the Athenian Agora came to an abrupt end in the year 267 A.D. when the Herulians, a tribe of barbarians from the northeast, successfully attacked Athens and withdrew, leaving the lower city a mass of smouldering ruins. In the Agora only the temple of Hephaistos escaped destruction; the useless remains of the other buildings were gathered as ready material for a new fortification encircling a small area immediately to the north of the Acropolis, a minute fraction of the original extent of the city.

Column drums, capitals and frieze blocks found their way into the wall without any attempt to dress them down to uniformity, while marble statues and especially heads were tossed into the lime kiln to provide mortar.

For a century and a half the Agora was a place of desolation. The splendid public buildings of an earlier age had given way to a scattering of primitive dwellings, and the activity of a sophisticated public life was replaced by the stoking of furnaces to melt down works of art for utilitarian purposes and by the grinding of olive presses.

2. A Water Mill at the Southeast Corner of the Agora, 5th–6th century A.D.

3. Lower Part of an Olive Mill.

4. Bed of an Oil Press.

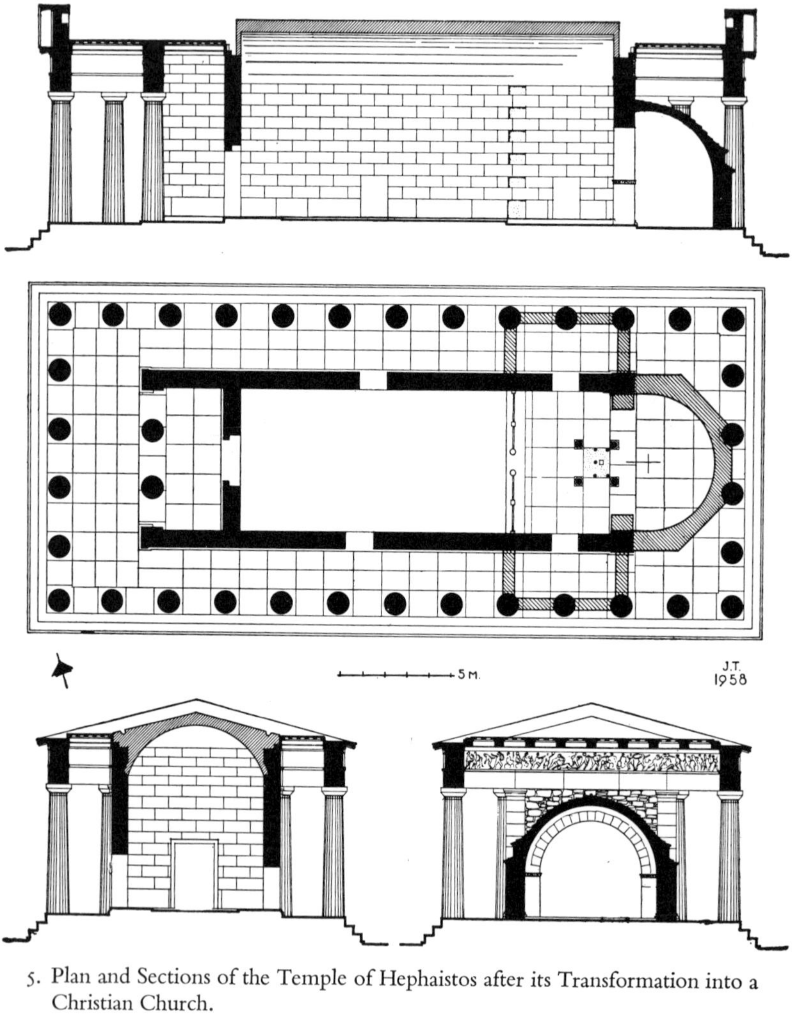

5. Plan and Sections of the Temple of Hephaistos after its Transformation into a Christian Church.

6. The Temple of Hephaistos from the Southwest.

Converted temples afforded places of worship for the Athenians of the 5th century A.D. onward. The temple of Hephaistos became the Church of St. George. Its entrance was changed from east to west to conform to Christian practice and an apse was built into the east end. The piers supporting the apse were crowned by new capitals carved with a cross as the central element of the design.

7. Early Christian Capital from the Church of St. George (Hephaisteion). A 3301.

8. A Capital from the Gymnasium. A 2268. The freshness of the carving reflects the short life of the building in which it was used.

With the threat of new raids a constant menace, there was little incentive for construction. Little by little, however, the barbarians were brought temporarily under control and the Athenians ventured outside the circumscribed area where they had taken refuge. Once more the ruins provided building material and a sprawling complex with a gymnasium, bath and numerous smaller rooms grew up on top of the earlier buildings. But the new edifice, which may perhaps have housed one or more of the schools of philosophy in Athens, had a short life and by the end of the 6th century it had gone out of use. Its end may have been hastened by the edict of the Emperor Justinian in 529 closing the schools of Athens.

9. A Statue of an Official of the 5th century A.D. S 697. It probably stood in the Gymnasium complex.

Paganism died hard in Athens and the gods were not easily superseded by saints and martyrs. Poseidon (right) is a more familiar figure even in the 5th century than St. Peter (below).

10. Lamp with Poseidon. L 5246.

11. Lamp with St. Peter? L 4754.

12. Leaf and Dart Moulding on Altar of Zeus Agoraios. 4th century B.C.

Classical models retained their popularity through the Early Christian period, but although the motifs were the same the plasticity of the classical gave way to a flatness of treatment which became more and more pronounced.

13. Early Christian Leaf and Dart. A 3058.

14. Ancient Capitals from the Holy Apostles.

Later builders preferred not to quarry or carve new blocks if old ones could be adapted to their purposes. Especially in Early Christian times, when many of the classical buildings of the Agora were lying in ruins, it was seldom necessary to look far for usable columns or capitals, since absolute uniformity was not regarded as essential.

The two capitals above were re-used in the 11th century church of the Holy Apostles; one is the conventional late Corinthian type, the other a modified form with an upper register of water leaves, first used in the near-by Tower of the Winds and much copied in later times.

An innovation of the Early Christian period was the impost capital, an ordinary capital with an additional member on top to provide the extra space necessitated by the use of arches instead of flat architraves.

15. Early Christian Impost Capital. A 3212.

16. Capital and Impost Block from the Areopagus. A 408 and A 409.

Although the period between the end of classical civilization and the fully developed Byzantine Empire is often regarded as the Dark Ages, some light flickered. The capital (above) and the closure slab from an altar screen (below) were found close to each other on the Areopagus and may perhaps be associated with the church of St. Dionysios the Areopagite, St. Paul's first convert in Athens. The actual date of the church is unknown but these architectural fragments may be dated in or about the 8th century.

17. Closure Slab from the Areopagus. S 487.

As the interests of the Empire, both political and commercial, became more and more identified with the East, classical motifs become rarer and less recognizable, while oriental influences were in the ascendant. Characteristic of this trend is a carved slab now built into the west façade of the 'Little Metropolis' (Gorgoepikoos) in Athens but brought there from some earlier building. On it two sphinxes are grouped heraldically to either side of a Tree of Life. Under the influence of textiles, one of the most sought after and easily transported commodities, all empty spaces are filled with ornamental designs.

18. Sculptured Slab in West Façade of Little Metropolis. 10th century.

19. Byzantine Sgraffito Plate of the 11th century. P 5026.

The green-glazed plate above owes little to the classical tradition. To the two-dimensional textile quality of the over-all pattern is added the border of imitation 'Kufic' writing, an ornamental form of Arabic script said to have been developed in the city of Kufa (Iraq) and much copied or adapted in 11th century Greece. Byzantine potters drew heavily on Islamic artists for inspiration.

20. Carved Lintel. 11th century. S 601.

One of the most popular books in the Middle Ages was the Bestiary: moral tales about animals real and fabulous. Their decorative and symbolic qualities combined well to make suitable subjects for architectural ornament or the lowlier potter's art.

21. Sgraffito Plate with Griffin. 12 century. P 2221.

22. Closure Slab with Peacocks. S 740.

23. P 7133.

24. P 14999.

25. P 14674.

26. P 12319.

Creatures such as these adorned the ordinary table wares of the 11th and 12th centuries. The Sgraffito technique called for little skill in drawing. The lines were scratched through a white surface wash into the dark clay beneath. The whole was then covered with a transparent yellow or green glaze so that the design stood out in dark against a light background.

27. P 10638.

28. P 2920.

29. P 8003.

30. P 3769.

A favorite legend in the Byzantine world concerned the hero Digenis Akritas, whose exploits are recounted in an epic and in numerous songs from all parts of the Empire. A guardian of the frontiers, slayer of bears, lions and dragons, comforter of ladies in distress, Digenis appears frequently on pottery of the 12th century; his portrait may perhaps be recognized on the plate below, with the 'blond curly hair and large, black-browed eyes' attributed to him in the epic.

31. Sgraffito Plate. 12th century. P 9396.

32. Sgraffito Plate. 12th century. P 8623.

More explicit is a song describing how Digenis slew a dragon by means of five arrows. Here the artist, or potter, has taken pains to make the scene unmistakable by clearly indicating the five arrows in the neck. In the warrior's left hand may be discerned the 'damascene sword' with which the *coup de grace* was given, according to the same song.

33. Incised Plate. 12th century. Corinth Museum. No. 1685.

A more peaceful episode in the life of Digenis is shown on a plate from Corinth. Returning through the desert from some exploit, the hero came upon a princess who had been abandoned by her lover, one of her father's prisoners with whom she had eloped. To cap his heartless behavior the erstwhile prisoner had taken with him not only the gold which the couple had stolen from the father but also the horse.

Again the scene is pin-pointed: the crown indicates the young lady's rank, and the 'low stool' on which, according to the epic, Digenis and the princess sat together before taking their leave on the hero's horse is clearly visible. In the field the rabbit, age-old symbol of love, serves also as a space-filler.

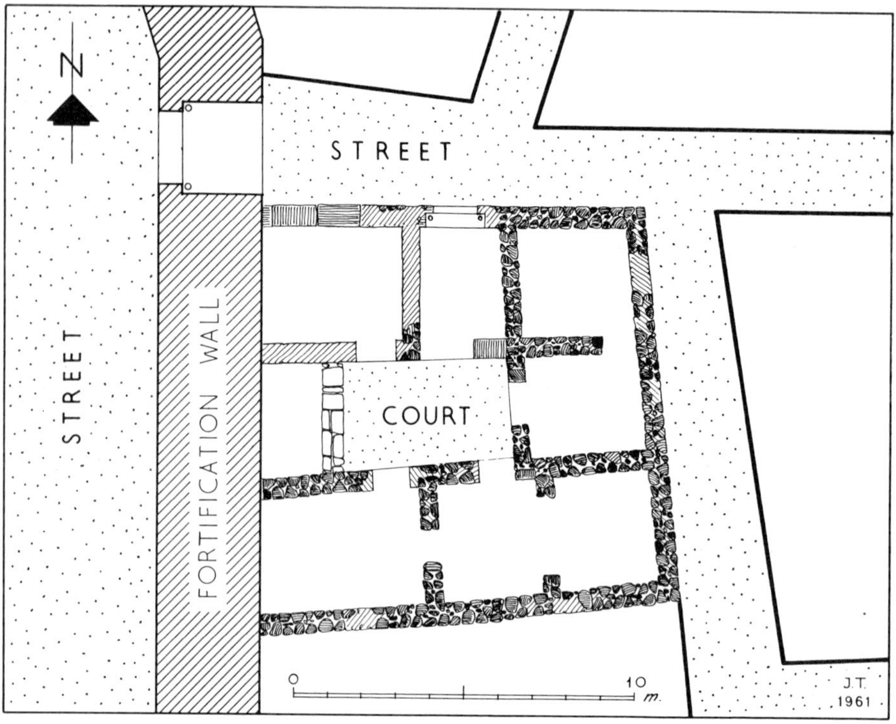

34. House Plan of the 12th century.

During the Middle Ages the whole area of the Agora was filled with private houses. Their plans were simple, not unlike those of the 5th century B.C., with a group of modest rooms surrounding a courtyard. A feature of nearly every house was the large storage jar (pithos) for oil or grain, buried in the earth up to its neck and covered with a square stone slab. The hole in the middle of the slab was for lifting, or perhaps for ventilation.

Pots and dishes such as those shown on the opposite page were used in these houses. 10th–11th centuries.

35. Storage Jars.

36. Green-Glazed Table Brazier. P 3075.

37. Brown-Glazed Brazier. P 10147.

38. Lamp. L 1680

39. Glass Cup. G 61.

40. Spouted Cooking Pot. P 10148.

41. Bronze Ornament. B 304.

42. Coin of Leo VI and Alexander, 886–912.

43. Bronze Cross. B 293.

Articles of adornment usually had a religious significance. St. George or one of the other equestrian saints or the Virgin Mary or a simple cross were common pendants.

Below, a bread stamp, probably to be used on the Eucharistic bread.

44. Bronze Ornament. B 674.

45. Bread Stamp. MC 74.

46. The Holy Apostles before Restoration.

The continuity of life is well illustrated in the Church of the Holy Apostles, which stands above the southeast corner of the ancient Agora. It owes its good state of preservation to the solid concrete foundations of the Roman fountain house on which it was built in the early years of the 11th century. The structure itself carries evidence of vicissitude through war, decay, remodelling and sometimes disastrous efforts toward beautification over a period of nine centuries.

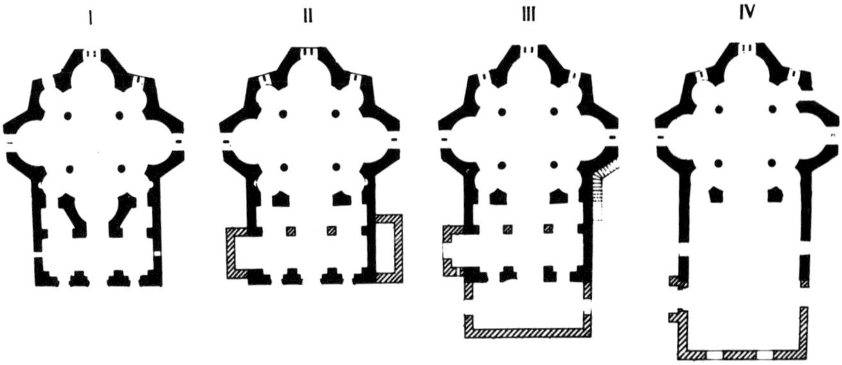

47. Four Stages in the Plan of the Church from the 11th to the 19th centuries.

48. The Holy Apostles after Removal of Late Additions.

Gunfire destroyed the western end of the church, probably in the 17th century. One of the cannon balls responsible for the destruction was found in a tomb beneath the ruined western apse.

The church was restored in 1954–56 through the generosity of the Samuel H. Kress Foundation.

49. The Church during the Reconstruction of the Narthex.

50. Laying the Floor Panel under the Dome.

51. A Fragment of an Original Closure Slab of the Altar Screen.

Marble fragments built into the later addition to the church or found in the vicinity provided models for the restored altar screen and other decorative details.

52. Two pieces of the Lintel of the Altar Screen.

53. Carving the Lunette for the Central Door.

54. The Dome before Restoration. Alternate windows had been blocked up and the arches of the others lowered and flattened.

55. (Opposite) The Dome after Restoration. The original brick window frames were still in place under the coating of stucco.

56. St. Romanus. A fresco of the 17th century in a niche near the narthex.

57. The Holy Apostles. Interior after Restoration.

58. The Holy Apostles. Exterior after Restoration.

59. Marble Sarcophagus Front. 13th century. S 511.

In 1204, Greece entered on a period of foreign occupation which was to last over six centuries. The Latin Crusaders, enticed by the riches of Constantinople, diverted the Fourth Crusade to attack the Byzantine capital. Into the Latin Kingdom of Constantinople was incorporated Greece, which was ruled by a succession of French, Spanish and Italian princes until its conquest by the Turks in 1456.

The sarcophagus above probably dates from the early years of the Latin occupation, but it was made by local artisans.

Below, the official seal of one of the last bishops of independent Athens, John VI, who was in office from 1180 to 1182.

60. Seal of Bishop John VI. 1180–1182. IL 360.

61. Imitation Majolica Jug. 16th century. P 1902.

62. Italian Bowl. 16th century. P 5673.

Trade with the West was reflected in some of the pottery of later times found in the Agora. The bowl above, with a Venetian Doge seated in his palace, was made in North Italy in the 16th century, while the lion opposite is a local imitation of Italian majolica of the 16th or 17th century. The lion may indeed be a product of the Athenian Agora, for kilns manufacturing such ware have been found in the area.

63. Venetian Ducat of Silvestro Valerio, 1694–1700.

64. SS. Blaisios and Eleutherios. Fresco from the 17th century Church of St. Spiridon (now in the Church of the Holy Apostles). The Church of St. Spiridon stood near the south end of the Stoa of Attalos.

65. A street near the Agora in Turkish times as seen by the English traveler Edward Dodwell in 1805. (*Views of Greece*, 1821)